LEADERSHIP

101

LEADERSHIP

WHAT EVERY LEADER NEEDS TO KNOW

JOHN C. MAXWELL

THOMAS NELSON PUBLISHERS®
Nashville

A Division of Thomas Nelson, Inc.
www.ThomasNelson.com

Published in Nashville, Tennessee, by Thomas Nelson, Inc.

Portions of this book were previously published in *Becoming a Person of
Influence, The 21 Irrefutable Laws of Leadership, The 21 Indispensable
Qualities of a Leader*, and *Developing the Leader Within You*.

Library of Congress Cataloging-in-Publication

Maxwell, John C., 1947–
Leadership 101 / John C. Maxwell.
p. cm.
ISBN 0-7852-6419-1 (hc)
1. Leadership. I. Title: Leadership one hundred one. II. Title.
HM1261 .M3897 2002
303.3'4—dc21
2002009572

Printed in the United States of America

04 05 06 PHX 16 15 14

CONTENTS

WHY LEADERSHIP 101?

Welcome to Leadership 101. You may be wondering why I'm doing another book on leadership. Let me tell you a story that will explain how *Leadership 101* came about and why we're doing it.

Every year I am invited to speak to the employees of Thomas Nelson Publishers in Nashville, Tennessee, and I am delighted to do it. I consider my publishers to be partners with me, and for a decade Thomas Nelson has been a good partner.

During my most recent visit, I got to speak to all of the publisher's employees, from presidents to warehouse workers, and I explained to them why I write books. I do it because I want to help people be successful. And I believe that to be a success in life, a person needs to be able to master skills in four areas: Relationships, Equipping, Attitude, and

Leadership. Those are the four subjects I write books about, and that's why I say that anyone can be a REAL success.

After I was done speaking, Mike Hyatt, the publisher of Thomas Nelson, and Pete Nikolai, the vice president of backlist development, came up to me and said, "John, people are always asking for small books that they can read in one sitting. You really ought to do a short easy-to-read book on each of those subjects. And you should start with the subject that put your books on *The New York Times* and *Business Week* bestsellers lists—leadership."

What they said is really true. People's lives are hectic, their time is valuable, and at the same time they are on information overload. Did you know that more new information has been produced in the last thirty years than in the previous 5,000? A weekday edition of *The New York Times* contains more information than average people in seventeenth century England were likely to come across in their lifetime. The amount of information available in the world has doubled in the last five years, and it keeps doubling.

That's why we've introduced *Leadership 101*. It's the first in a series of four books that gives you the "short course" on what it takes to become a REAL success. In *Leadership 101*, I've collected what you need to know for the bottom line on leadership. This book contains the essentials gained from more than thirty years of leadership experience. It defines leadership, identifies a few traits every leader should develop, and shows the impact leadership can have on your life and the lives of those you lead.

Did you know that each of us influences at least ten thousand other people during our lifetime? So the question is not *whether* you will influence someone, but *how* you will use your influence. This book is designed to help you develop your leadership ability and increase your personal and organizational success. Whether your desire is to build a business, strengthen your children, or reach the world, the first step in achieving it is raising your level of leadership.

Sir Francis Bacon observed that knowledge is power. Back when he lived and information was scarce, that may have been true. But today, it would be better to say that knowledge empowers—as long as it's what you need. My desire is to empower you and to see you at the next level.

PART I

THE DEVELOPMENT OF A LEADER

I

WHY SHOULD I GROW AS A LEADER?

*The higher the leadership,
the greater the effectiveness.*

I often open my leadership conferences by explaining what I call the Law of the Lid because it helps people understand the value of leadership. If you can get a handle on this principle, you will see the incredible impact of leadership on every aspect of life. So here it is: Leadership ability is the lid that determines a person's level of effectiveness. The lower an individual's ability to lead, the lower the lid on his potential. The higher the leadership, the greater the effectiveness. To give you an example, if your leadership rates an 8, then your effectiveness can never be greater than a 7. If your leadership is only a 4, then your effectiveness will be no higher than a 3. Your leadership ability—for better or for worse—always determines your effectiveness and the potential impact of your organization.

Let me tell you a story that illustrates the Law of the Lid.

In 1930, two young brothers named Dick and Maurice moved from New Hampshire to California in search of the American Dream. They had just gotten out of high school, and they saw few opportunities back home. So they headed straight for Hollywood where they eventually found jobs on a movie studio set.

After a while, their entrepreneurial spirit and interest in the entertainment industry prompted them to open a theater in Glendale, a town about five miles northeast of Hollywood. But despite all their efforts, the brothers just couldn't make the business profitable, so they looked for a better business opportunity.

A NEW OPPORTUNITY

In 1937, the brothers opened a small drive-in restaurant in Pasadena, located just east of Glendale. As people in southern California became more dependent on their cars in the thirties, drive-in restaurants sprang up everywhere. Customers would drive into a parking lot around a small restaurant, place their orders with carhops, and receive their food on trays right in their cars. The food was served on china plates complete with glassware and metal utensils.

Dick and Maurice's tiny drive-in restaurant was a great success, and in 1940, they moved the operation to San

Bernardino, a working-class boomtown fifty miles east of Los Angeles. They built a larger facility and expanded their menu from hot dogs, fries, and shakes to include barbecued beef and pork sandwiches, hamburgers, and other items. Their business exploded. Annual sales reached $200,000, and the brothers found themselves splitting $50,000 in profits every year—a sum that put them in the town's financial elite.

By 1948, their intuition told them that times were changing, so they made modifications to their restaurant business. They eliminated the carhops and started serving only walk-up customers. They reduced their menu and focused on selling hamburgers. They eliminated plates, glassware, and metal utensils, switching to paper products instead. They reduced their costs and the prices they charged customers. They also created what they called the Speedy Service System. Their kitchen became like an assembly line, where each person focused on service with speed. Their goal was to fill each customer's order in thirty seconds or less. And they succeeded. By the mid-1950s, annual revenue hit $350,000, and by then, Dick and Maurice split net profits of about $100,000 each year.

Who were these brothers? On the front of their small restaurant hung a neon sign that said simply MCDONALD'S HAMBURGERS. Dick and Maurice McDonald had hit the great American jackpot, and the rest, as they say, is history, right? Wrong. The McDonalds never went any farther because their weak leadership put a lid on their ability to succeed.

THE STORY BEHIND THE STORY

It's true that the McDonald brothers were financially secure. Theirs was one of the most profitable restaurant enterprises in the country, and their genius was in customer service and kitchen organization, which led to a new system of food and beverage service. In fact, their talent was so widely known in food service circles that people from all over the country wanted to learn more about their methods. At one point, they received as many as three hundred calls and letters every month. That led them to the idea of marketing the McDonald's concept.

The idea of franchising restaurants had been around for several decades. To the McDonald brothers, it looked like a way to make money without having to open another restaurant themselves. In 1952, they tried it, but their effort was a dismal failure. The reason was simple: They lacked the leadership necessary to make it effective.

Dick and Maurice were good restaurant owners. They understood how to run a business, make their systems efficient, cut costs, and increase profits. They were efficient managers. But they were not leaders. Their thinking patterns clamped a lid down on what they could do and become. At the height of their success, Dick and Maurice found themselves smack-dab against the Law of the Lid.

THE BROTHERS PARTNER WITH A LEADER

In 1954, the brothers hooked up with a man named Ray Kroc who *was* a leader. Kroc had been running a small company he founded, which sold machines for making milk shakes. McDonald's was one of his best customers, and as soon as he visited the store, he had a vision for its potential. In his mind he could see the restaurant going nationwide in hundreds of markets. He soon struck a deal with Dick and Maurice, and in 1955, he formed McDonald's System, Inc. (later called the McDonald's Corporation).

Kroc immediately bought the rights to a franchise so that he could use it as a model and prototype to sell other franchises. Then he began to assemble a team and build an organization to make McDonald's a nationwide entity.

In the early years, Kroc sacrificed a lot. Though he was in his midfifties, he worked long hours just as he had when he first got started in business thirty years earlier. He eliminated many frills at home, including his country club membership, which he later said added ten strokes to his golf game. During his first eight years with McDonald's, he took no salary. He also personally borrowed money from the bank and against his life insurance to help cover the salaries of a few key leaders he wanted on the team. His sacrifice and his leadership paid off. In 1961 for the sum of $2.7 million, Kroc bought the exclusive rights to McDonald's from the brothers, and he proceeded to turn it into an American institution and global entity. The "lid" in the life and leadership of Ray Kroc was obviously much higher than that of his predecessors.

In the years that Dick and Maurice McDonald had attempted to franchise their food service system, they managed to sell the concept to just fifteen buyers, only ten of whom actually opened restaurants. On the other hand, the leadership lid in Ray Kroc's life was sky high. Between 1955 and 1959, Kroc succeeded in opening 100 restaurants. Four years after that, there were 500 McDonald's. Today the company has opened more than 21,000 restaurants in no fewer than 100 countries.[1] Leadership ability—or more specifically the lack of leadership ability—was the lid on the McDonald brothers' effectiveness.

SUCCESS WITHOUT LEADERSHIP

I believe that success is within the reach of just about everyone. But I also believe that personal success without leadership ability brings only limited effectiveness. A person's impact is only a fraction of what it could be with good leadership. The higher you want to climb, the more you need leadership. The greater the impact you want to make, the greater your influence needs to be. Whatever you will accomplish is restricted by your ability to lead others.

Let me give you a picture of what I mean. Let's say that when it comes to success, you're an 8 (on a scale from 1 to 10). That's pretty good. I think it would be safe to say that the McDonald brothers were in that range. But let's also say that your leadership ability is only a 1. Your level of effectiveness would look like this:

SUCCESS WITHOUT LEADERSHIP

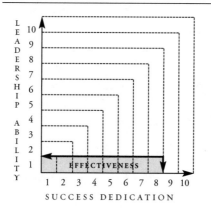

To increase your level of effectiveness, you have a couple of choices. You could work very hard to increase your dedication to success and excellence—to work toward becoming a 10. It's possible that you could make it to that level, though the law of diminishing returns says that your success will increase only to a certain point, after which, it fails to increase in proportion to the amount of work you put into it. In other words, the effort it would take to increase those last two points might take more energy than it did to achieve the first eight. If you really killed yourself, you might increase your success by that 25 percent.

But you have another option. Let's say that instead you work hard to increase your level of *leadership*. Over the course of time, you develop yourself as a leader, and eventually, your leadership ability becomes, say, a 6. Visually, the results would look like the chart on the opposite page.

By raising your leadership ability—without increasing your success dedication at all—you can increase your original effectiveness by 500 percent! If you were to raise your leadership to 8, where it matched your success dedication, you would increase your effectiveness by 700 percent! Leadership has a multiplying effect. I've seen its impact over and over again in all kinds of businesses and nonprofit organizations. And that's why I've taught leadership for more than twenty-five years.

SUCCESS WITH LEADERSHIP

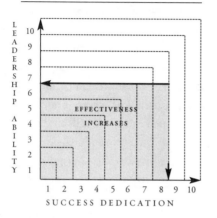

TO CHANGE THE DIRECTION OF THE ORGANIZATION, CHANGE THE LEADER

Leadership ability is always the lid on personal and organizational effectiveness. If the leadership is strong, the lid is high. But if it's not, then the organization is limited. That's why in times of trouble, organizations naturally look for new leadership. When the country is experiencing hard times, it elects a new president. When a church is floundering, it searches for a new senior pastor. When a sports team keeps losing, it looks for a new head coach. When a company is losing money, it hires a new CEO.

A few years ago, I met Don Stephenson, the chairman of Global Hospitality Resources, Inc., of San Diego, California, an international hospitality advisory and consulting firm. Over lunch, I asked him about his organization. Today he primarily does consulting, but back then his company took over the management of hotels and resorts that weren't doing well financially. They oversaw many excellent facilities such as La Costa in southern California.

TO REACH THE HIGHEST LEVEL OF EFFECTIVENESS, YOU
HAVE TO RAISE THE LID OF LEADERSHIP ABILITY.

Don said that whenever they came into an organization to take it over, they always started by doing two things: First, they trained all the staff to improve their level of service to the customers, and second, they fired the leader. When he told me that, I was at first surprised.

"You *always* fire him?" I asked. "Every time?"

"That's right. Every time," he said.

"Don't you talk to the person first—to check him out to see if he's a good leader?" I said.

"No," he answered. "If he'd been a good leader, the organization wouldn't be in the mess it's in."

And I thought to myself, *Of course. It's the Law of the Lid.* To reach the highest level of effectiveness, you have to raise the lid—one way or another.

The good news is that getting rid of the leader isn't the *only* way. Just as I teach in conferences that there is a lid, I also teach that you can raise it.

2

___

How Can I Grow as a Leader?

*Leadership develops daily,
not in a day.*

Becoming a leader is a lot like investing successfully in the stock market. If your hope is to make a fortune in a day, you're not going to be successful. What matters most is what you do day by day over the long haul. My friend Tag Short maintains, "The secret of our success is found in our daily agenda." If you continually invest in your leadership development, letting your "assets" compound, the inevitable result is growth over time.

When I teach leadership at conferences, people inevitably ask me whether leaders are born. I always answer, "Yes, of course they are . . . I've yet to meet one that came into the world any other way!" We all laugh, and then I answer the real question—whether leadership is something a person either possesses or doesn't.

Although it's true that some people are born with greater

12

natural gifts than others, the ability to lead is really a collection of skills, nearly all of which can be learned and improved. But that process doesn't happen overnight. Leadership is complicated. It has many facets: respect, experience, emotional strength, people skills, discipline, vision, momentum, timing—the list goes on. As you can see, many factors that come into play in leadership are intangible. That's why leaders require so much seasoning to be effective. It was around the time I turned fifty that I truly began to understand the many aspects of leadership with clarity.

THE FOUR PHASES OF LEADERSHIP GROWTH

Whether you do or don't have great natural ability for leadership, your development and progress will probably occur according to the following four phases:

PHASE 1—I DON'T KNOW WHAT I DON'T KNOW

Most people fail to recognize the value of leadership. They believe that leadership is only for a few—for the people at the top of the corporate ladder. They have no idea of the opportunities they're passing up when they don't learn to lead. This point was driven home for me when a college president shared with me that only a handful of students signed up for a leadership course offered by the school. Why? Only a few thought of themselves as leaders. If they had known that leadership is influence, and that in the course of each day most individuals usually try to influence at least four other people, their desire might have been sparked to learn more about the subject. It's unfortunate because as long as a person doesn't know what he doesn't know, he doesn't grow.

PHASE 2—I KNOW WHAT I DON'T KNOW

Usually at some point in life, we are placed in a leadership position only to look around and discover that no one is following us. That's when we realize that we need to *learn* how to lead. And of course, that's when it's possible for the process to start. English Prime Minister Benjamin Disraeli wisely commented, "To be conscious that you are ignorant of the facts is a great step to knowledge."

SUCCESSFUL LEADERS ARE LEARNERS. AND THE
LEARNING PROCESS IS ONGOING, A RESULT OF
SELF-DISCIPLINE AND PERSEVERANCE.

That's what happened to me when I took my first leadership position in 1969. I had captained sports teams all my life and had been the student government president in college, so I already thought I was a leader. But when I tried to lead people in the real world, I found out the awful truth. That prompted me to start gathering resources and learning from them. I also had another idea: I wrote to the top ten leaders in my field and offered them one hundred dollars for a half hour of their time so that I could ask them questions. (That was quite a sum for me in 1969.) For the next several years, my wife, Margaret, and I planned every vacation around where those people lived. If a great leader in Cleveland said yes to my request, then that year we vacationed in Cleveland so that I could meet him. And my idea really paid off. Those men shared insights with me that I could have learned no other way.

Phase 3—I Grow and Know and It Starts to Show

When you recognize your lack of skill and begin the daily discipline of personal growth in leadership, exciting things start to happen.

Awhile back I was teaching a group of people in Denver, and in the crowd I noticed a really sharp nineteen-year-old named Brian. For a couple of days, I watched as he eagerly took notes. I talked to him a few times during breaks. When I got to the part of the seminar where I emphasize that leadership is a process, I asked Brian to stand up so that I could talk while everyone listened. I said, "Brian, I've been watching you here, and I'm very impressed with how hungry you are to learn and glean and grow. I want to tell you a secret that will change your life." Everyone in the whole auditorium seemed to lean forward.

"I believe that in about twenty years, you can be a *great* leader. I want to encourage you to make yourself a lifelong learner of leadership. Read books, listen to tapes regularly, and keep attending seminars. And whenever you come across a golden nugget of truth or a significant quote, file it away for the future.

"It's not going to be easy," I said. "But in five years, you'll see progress as your influence becomes greater. In ten years you'll develop a competence that makes your leadership highly effective. And in twenty years, when you're only thirty-nine years old, if you've continued to learn and grow, others will likely start asking you to teach them about leadership. And some will be amazed. They'll look at each other and say, 'How did he suddenly become so wise?'

"Brian, you can be a great leader, but it won't happen in a day. Start paying the price now."

What's true for Brian is also true for you. Start developing your leadership today, and someday you will experience the effects of this process.

PHASE 4—I SIMPLY GO BECAUSE OF WHAT I KNOW

When you're in phase 3, you can be pretty effective as a leader, but you have to think about every move you make. However, when you get to phase 4, your ability to lead becomes almost automatic. And that's when the payoff is larger than life. But the only way to get there is to recognize the process and pay the price.

TO LEAD TOMORROW, LEARN TODAY

Leadership is developed daily, not in a day—that is reality. The good news is that your leadership ability is not static. No matter where you're starting from, you can get better. That's true even for people who have stood on the world stage of leadership. While most presidents of the United States reach their peak while in office, others continue to grow and become better leaders afterward, such as former president Jimmy Carter. Some people questioned his ability to lead while in the White House. But in recent years, Carter's level of influence has continually increased. His high integrity and dedication in serving people through Habitat for Humanity and other organizations have made his influence grow. People are now truly impressed with his life.

FIGHTING YOUR WAY UP

There is an old saying: Champions don't become champions in the ring—they are merely recognized there. That's true. If you want to see where someone develops into a champion, look at his daily routine. Former heavyweight champ Joe Frazier stated, "You can map out a fight plan or a life plan. But when the action starts, you're down to your reflexes. That's where your road work shows. If you cheated on that in the dark of the morning, you're getting found out now under the bright lights."[1] Boxing is a good analogy for leadership development because it is all about daily preparation. Even if a person has natural talent, he has to prepare and train to become successful.

One of this country's greatest leaders was a fan of boxing: President Theodore Roosevelt. In fact, one of his most famous quotes uses a boxing analogy:

> It is not the critic who counts, not the man who points out how the strong man stumbled, or where the doer of deeds could have done them better. The credit belongs to the man who is actually in the arena; whose face is marred by dust and sweat and blood; who strives valiantly; who errs and comes short again and again; who knows the great enthusiasms, the great

devotions, and spends himself in a worthy cause; who, at best, knows in the end the triumph of high achievement; and who, at the worst, if he fails, at least fails while daring greatly, so that his place shall never be with those cold and timid souls who know neither victory nor defeat.

A boxer himself, Roosevelt was not only an effective leader, but he was the most flamboyant of all U.S. presidents.

A Man of Action

TR (which was Roosevelt's nickname) was known for regular boxing and judo sessions, challenging horseback rides, and long, strenuous hikes. A French ambassador who visited Roosevelt used to tell about the time that he accompanied the president on a walk through the woods. When the two men came to the banks of a stream that was too deep to cross by foot, TR stripped off his clothes and expected the dignitary to do the same so that they could swim to the other side. Nothing was an obstacle to Roosevelt.

His enthusiasm and stamina seemed boundless. As the vice presidential candidate in 1900, he gave 673 speeches and traveled 20,000 miles while campaigning for President

McKinley. And years after his presidency, while preparing to deliver a speech in Milwaukee, Roosevelt was shot in the chest by a would-be assassin. With a broken rib and a bullet in his chest, Roosevelt insisted on delivering his one-hour speech before allowing himself to be taken to the hospital.

ROOSEVELT STARTED SLOW

Of all the leaders this nation has ever had, Roosevelt was one of the toughest—both physically and mentally. But he didn't start that way. America's cowboy president was born in Manhattan to a prominent wealthy family. As a child, he was puny and very sickly. He had debilitating asthma, possessed very poor eyesight, and was painfully thin. His parents weren't sure he would survive.

When he was twelve, young Roosevelt's father told him, "You have the mind, but you have not the body, and without the help of the body the mind cannot go as far as it should. You must *make* the body." And make it he did. TR began spending time *every day* building his body as well as his mind, and he did that for the rest of his life. He worked out with weights, hiked, ice-skated, hunted, rowed, rode horseback, and boxed. By the time TR graduated from Harvard, he was ready to tackle the world of politics.

No Overnight Success

Roosevelt didn't become a great leader overnight, either. His road to the presidency was one of slow, continual growth. As he served in various positions, ranging from New York City Police Commissioner to President of the United States, he kept learning and growing. He improved himself, and in time he became a strong leader.

Roosevelt's list of accomplishments is remarkable. Under his leadership, the United States emerged as a world power. He helped the country develop a first-class navy. He saw that the Panama Canal was built. He negotiated peace between Russia and Japan, winning a Nobel Peace Prize in the process. And when people questioned TR's leadership—since he had become president when McKinley was assassinated—he campaigned and was reelected by the largest majority of any president up to his time.

Ever the man of action, when Roosevelt completed his term as president in 1909, he immediately traveled to Africa where he led a scientific expedition sponsored by the Smithsonian Institution.

On January 6, 1919, at his home in New York, Theodore Roosevelt died in his sleep. Then Vice President Marshall said, "Death had to take him sleeping, for if Roosevelt had been awake, there would have been a fight." When they removed him from his bed, they found a book under his pillow. Up to the very last, TR was still striving to learn and improve himself.

If you want to be a leader, the good news is that you can do it. Everyone has the potential, but it isn't accomplished overnight. It requires perseverance. And you absolutely cannot ignore that becoming a leader is a process. Leadership doesn't develop in a day. It takes a lifetime.

PART 2

THE TRAITS OF
A LEADER

3

How Can I Become Disciplined?

The first person you lead is you.

It's a tough road to the top. Not many people ever reach the place where they are considered one of the best at their work. And even fewer are believed to be *the* best—ever. Yet that's what Jerry Rice has achieved. He is called the best person ever to play wide receiver in football. And he has got the records to prove it.

People who know him well say he is a natural. Physically his God-given gifts are incredible, yet those alone have not made him great. The real key to his success has been his self-discipline. He works and prepares—day in and day out—unlike anyone else in professional football.

During practice in high school, Rice's coach, Charles Davis, made his players sprint twenty times up and down a forty-yard hill. On a particularly hot and muggy Mississippi day, Rice was ready to give up after eleven trips. As he sneaked toward the locker room, he realized what he was doing.

"Don't quit," he told himself. "Because once you get into that mode of quitting, then you feel like it's okay." He went back and finished his sprints, and he has never been a quitter since.

As a professional player, he has become famous for his ability to sprint up another hill—a rugged 2.5-mile park trail in San Carlos, California—that Rice makes a regular part of his workout schedule. Other top players try to keep up with him on it, but they fall behind, astounded by his stamina. But that's only a part of Rice's regular routine. Even in the off-season, while other players are fishing or lying around enjoying downtime, Rice is working, his normal exercise routine lasting from 7:00 A.M. to noon. Someone once joked, "He is so well-conditioned that he makes Jamie Lee Curtis look like James Earl Jones."

"What a lot of guys don't understand about Jerry is that with him, football's a twelve-month thing," says NFL cornerback Kevin Smith. "He's a natural, but he still works. That's what separates the good from the great."

NO MATTER HOW GIFTED A LEADER IS, HIS GIFTS WILL NEVER REACH THEIR MAXIMUM POTENTIAL WITHOUT THE APPLICATION OF SELF-DISCIPLINE.

In 1997, Rice climbed another hill in his career: he made a comeback from a devastating injury. Prior to that, he had never missed a game in nineteen seasons of football, a testament to his disciplined work ethic and absolute tenacity. When he blew out his knee on August 31, 1997, people thought he was finished for the season. After all, only one player had ever had a similar injury and come back in the same season—Rod Woodson. He had rehabilitated his knee in four and a half months. Rice did it in three and a half—through sheer grit, determination, and incredible self-discipline. People had never seen anything like it before, and they might not again. And Rice continues to build his records and his reputation while helping his team win.

A Disciplined Direction

Jerry Rice is a perfect example of the power of self-discipline. No one achieves and sustains success without it. And no matter how gifted a leader is, his gifts will never reach their maximum potential without the application of self-discipline. It positions a leader to go to the highest level and is a key to leadership that lasts.

If you want to become a leader for whom self-discipline is an asset, follow these action points:

Challenge Your Excuses

To develop a lifestyle of discipline, one of your first tasks must be to challenge and eliminate any tendency to make excuses. As French classical writer François La Rochefoucauld said, "Almost all our faults are more pardonable than the methods we think up to hide them." If you have several reasons why you can't be self-disciplined, realize that they are really just a bunch of excuses—all of which need to be challenged if you want to go to the next level as a leader.

REMOVE REWARDS UNTIL THE JOB IS DONE

Author Mike Delaney wisely remarked, "Any business or industry that pays equal rewards to its goof-offs and its eager-beavers sooner or later will find itself with more goof-offs than eager-beavers." If you lack self-discipline, you may be in the habit of having dessert before eating your vegetables.

A story illustrates the power of withholding rewards. An older couple had been at a campground for a couple of days when a family arrived at the site next to them. As soon as their sport-utility vehicle came to a stop, the couple and their three kids piled out. One child hurriedly unloaded ice chests, backpacks, and other items while the other two quickly put up tents. The site was ready in fifteen minutes.

The older couple was amazed. "You folks sure do work great together," the elderly gentleman told the dad admiringly.

"You just need a system," replied the dad. "Nobody goes to the bathroom until camp's set up."

STAY FOCUSED ON RESULTS

Anytime you concentrate on the difficulty of the work instead of its results or rewards, you're likely to become discouraged. Dwell on it too long, and you'll develop self-pity instead of self-discipline. The next time you're facing a must-do task and you're thinking of doing what's convenient instead of paying the price, change your focus. Count the benefits of doing what's right, and then dive in.

IF YOU KNOW YOU HAVE TALENT, AND YOU'VE SEEN A
LOT OF MOTION BUT LITTLE CONCRETE RESULTS—
YOU MAY LACK SELF-DISCIPLINE.

Author H. Jackson Brown Jr. quipped, "Talent without discipline is like an octopus on roller skates. There's plenty of movement, but you never know if it's going to be forward, backwards, or sideways." If you know you have talent, and you've seen a lot of motion—but little concrete results—you may lack self-discipline.

Look at last week's schedule. How much of your time did you devote to regular, disciplined activities? Did you do anything to grow and improve yourself professionally? Did you engage in activities promoting good health? Did you dedicate part of your income to savings or investments? If you've been putting off those things, telling yourself that you'll do them later, you may need to work on your self-discipline.

4

How Should I Prioritize My Life?

*The discipline to prioritize and the ability
to work toward a stated goal are essential
to a leader's success.*

Success can be defined as *the progressive realization of a predetermined goal*. This definition tells us that the discipline to prioritize and the ability to work toward a stated goal are essential to a leader's success. In fact, I believe they are the key to leadership.

Many years ago, while working toward a business degree, I learned about the Pareto Principle. It is commonly called the 20/80 principle. Although I received little information about this principle at the time, I began applying it to my life. Years later I find it is a most useful tool for determining priorities for any person's life or for any organization.

The Pareto Principle: The 20/80 Principle

Twenty percent of your priorities will give you 80 percent of your production, IF you spend your time, energy, money, and personnel on the top 20 percent of your priorities.

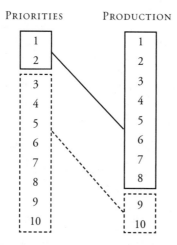

Priorities   Production

The solid lines on the illustration of the 20/80 Principle above represent a person or organization that spends time, energy, money, and personnel on the most important priorities. The result is a four-fold return in productivity. The dotted lines represent a person or organization that spends time, energy, money, and personnel on the lesser priorities. The result is a very small return.

EXAMPLES OF THE PARETO PRINCIPLE:

Time	20 percent of our time produces 80 percent of the results.
Counseling	20 percent of the people take up 80 percent of our time.
Products	20 percent of the products bring in 80 percent of the profit.
Reading	20 percent of the book contains 80 percent of the content.
Job	20 percent of our work gives us 80 percent of our satisfaction.
Speech	20 percent of the presentation produces 80 percent of the impact.
Donations	20 percent of the people will give 80 percent of the money.
Leadership	20 percent of the people will make 80 percent of the decisions.
Picnic	20 percent of the people will eat 80 percent of the food!

Every leader needs to understand the Pareto Principle in the area of people oversight and leadership. For example, 20 percent of the people in an organization will be responsible for 80 percent of the company's success. The following strategy will enable a leader to increase the productivity of an organization.

1. Determine which people are the top 20 percent producers.

2. Spend 80 percent of your "people time" with the top 20 percent.
3. Spend 80 percent of your personal development dollars on the top 20 percent.
4. Determine what 20 percent of the work gives 80 percent of the return and train an assistant to do the 80 percent less-effective work. This "frees up" the producer to do what he/she does best.
5. Ask the top 20 percent to do on-the-job training for the next 20 percent.

Remember, we teach what we know; we reproduce what we are. Like begets like. I teach this principle at leadership conferences, and I am often asked, "How do I identify the top 20 percent influencers/producers in my organization?" I suggest that you make a list of everyone in your company or department. Then ask yourself this question about each individual: "If this person takes a negative action against me or withdraws his or her support from me, what will the impact likely be?" If you won't be able to function, then put a check mark next to that name. If the person can help you or hurt you, but cannot make or break you in terms of your ability to get important things done, then don't put a check mark next to that name. When you get through making the check marks, you will have marked between 15 and 20 percent of the names. Those are the vital relationships that need to be developed and given the proper amount of resources needed to grow the organization.

ORGANIZE OR AGONIZE

Remember: It's not how hard you work; it's how smart you work. The ability to juggle three or four high priority projects successfully is a must for every leader.

A LIFE IN WHICH ANYTHING GOES WILL ULTIMATELY BE A LIFE IN WHICH NOTHING GOES.

Prioritize Assignments

High Importance/High Urgency: Tackle these projects first.

High Importance/Low Urgency: Set deadlines for completion and get these projects worked into your daily routine.

Low Importance/High Urgency: Find quick, efficient ways to get this work done without much personal involvement. If possible, delegate it to a "can do" assistant.

Low Importance/Low Urgency: This is busy or repetitious work, such as filing. Stack it up and do it in one-half hour segments every week; get somebody else to do it; or don't do it at all. Before putting off until tomorrow something you can do today, study it clearly. Maybe you can postpone it indefinitely.

CHOOSE OR LOSE

Every person is an initiator or reactor when it comes to planning. An example is our calendar. The question is not "Will my calendar be full?" but "Who will fill my calendar?" If we are leaders of others, the question is not "Will I see people?" but "Who will I see?" My observation is that leaders tend to initiate and followers tend to react. Note the difference:

LEADERS	FOLLOWERS
Initiate	React
Lead; pick up phone and make contact	Listen; wait for phone to ring
Spend time planning; anticipate problems	Spend time living day-to-day reacting to problems
Invest time with people	Spend time with people
Fill the calendar by priorities	Fill the calendar by requests

EVALUATE OR STALEMATE

Many times priorities are not black or white, but many tones of gray. I have found that the last thing one knows is what to put first. The following questions will assist your priority process:

What is required of me? A leader can give up anything except final responsibility. The question that must always be answered before accepting a new job is "What is required of me?" In other words, what do I have to do that no one but me can do? Whatever those things are, they must be put high on the priority list. Failure to do them will cause you to be among the unemployed. There will be many responsibilities of the levels under your position, but only a few that require you to be the one and only one who can do them. Distinguish between what you have to do and what can be delegated to someone else.

What gives me the greatest return? The effort expended should approximate the results expected. A question I must continually ask myself is, "Am I doing what I do best and receiving a good return for the organization?" Three common problems in many organizations are:

- Abuse: Too few employees are doing too much.
- Disuse: Too many employees are doing too little.
- Misuse: Too many employees are doing the wrong things.

What is most rewarding? Life is too short not to be fun. Our best work takes place when we enjoy it. Some time ago I spoke at a leaders' conference where I attempted to teach this principle. The title of my lecture was "Take This Job and Love It." I encouraged the audience to find something they liked to do so much they would gladly do it for nothing. Then I suggested they learn to do it so well that people would be happy to pay them for it. You enjoy yourself because you are making your contribution to the world.

Success in your work will be greatly increased if the three Rs—Requirements, Return, Reward—are similar. In other words, if the requirements of my job are the same as my strengths that give me the highest return and doing those things brings me great pleasure, then I will be successful if I act on my priorities.

PRIORITY PRINCIPLES

PRIORITIES NEVER "STAY PUT"

Priorities continually shift and demand attention. H. Ross Perot said that anything that is excellent or praiseworthy stands moment-by-moment on the cutting edge and must be constantly fought for. Well-placed priorities always sit on "the edge."

To keep priorities in place:

- Evaluate: Every month review the three Rs (Requirements/Return/Reward).
- Eliminate: Ask yourself, "What am I doing that can be done by someone else?"
- Estimate: What are the top projects you are doing this month and how long will they take?

YOU CANNOT OVERESTIMATE THE
UNIMPORTANCE OF PRACTICALLY EVERYTHING

I love this principle. It's a little exaggerated but needs to be said. William James said that the art of being wise is "the art of knowing what to overlook." The petty and the mundane steal much of our time. Too many are living for the wrong things.

Dr. Anthony Campolo tells about a sociological study in which fifty people over the age of ninety-five were asked one question: "If you could live your life over again, what would you do differently?" It was an open-ended question, and a multiplicity of answers came from these eldest of senior citizens. However, three answers constantly reemerged and dominated the results of the study. Those answers were:

- If I had it to do over again, I would reflect more.
- If I had it to do over again, I would risk more.
- If I had it to do over again, I would do more things that would live on after I am dead.

A young concert violinist was asked the secret of her success. She replied, "Planned neglect." Then she explained, "When I was in school, there were many things that demanded my time. When I went to my room after breakfast, I made my bed, straightened the room, dusted the floor, and did whatever else came to my attention. Then I hurried to my violin practice. I found I wasn't progressing as I thought I should, so I reversed things. Until my practice period was completed, I deliberately neglected everything else. That program of planned neglect, I believe, accounts for my success."[1]

THE GOOD IS THE ENEMY OF THE BEST

Most people can prioritize when faced with right or wrong issues. The challenge arises when we are faced with two good choices. Now what should we do? What if both choices fall comfortably into the requirements, return, and reward of our work?

How to Break the Tie Between Two Good Options

- Ask your overseer or coworkers their preference.
- Can one of the options be handled by someone else? If so, pass it on and work on the one only you can do.
- Which option would be of more benefit to the customer? Too many times we are like the merchant who was so intent on trying to keep the store clean that he would never unlock the front door. The real reason for running the store is to have customers come in, not to clean it up!
- Make your decision based on the purpose of the organization.

TOO MANY PRIORITIES PARALYZE US

Every one of us has looked at our desks filled with memos and papers, heard the phone ringing, and watched the door open all at the same time! Remember the "frozen feeling" that came over you?

William H. Hinson tells us why animal trainers carry a stool when they go into a cage of lions. They have their whips, of course, and their pistols are at their sides. But invariably they also carry a stool. Hinson says it is the most important tool of the trainer. He holds the stool by the back and thrusts the legs toward the face of the wild animal. Those who know maintain that the animal tries to focus on all four legs at once. In the attempt to focus on all four, a kind of paralysis overwhelms the animal, and it becomes tame, weak, and disabled because its attention is fragmented. (Now we will have more empathy for the lions.)

If you are overloaded with work, list the priorities on a separate sheet of paper *before* you take it to your boss and see what he will choose as the priorities.

The last of each month I plan and lay out my priorities for the next month. I sit down with my assistant and have her place those projects on the calendar. She handles hundreds of things for me on a monthly basis. However, when something is of High Importance/High Urgency, I communicate that to her so it will be placed above other things.

All true leaders have learned to say no to the good in order to say yes to the best.

WHEN LITTLE PRIORITIES DEMAND TOO MUCH OF US, BIG PROBLEMS ARISE

Robert J. McKain said, "The reason most major goals are not achieved is that we spend our time doing second things first."

EFFICIENCY IS THE FOUNDATION FOR SURVIVAL.
EFFECTIVENESS IS THE FOUNDATION FOR SUCCESS.

Often the little things in life trip us up. A tragic example is an Eastern Airlines jumbo jet that crashed in the Everglades of Florida. The plane was the now-famous Flight 401, bound from New York to Miami with a heavy load of holiday passengers. As the plane approached the Miami airport for its landing, the light that indicates proper deployment of the landing gear failed to light. The plane flew in a large, looping circle over the swamps of the Everglades while the cockpit crew checked to see if the gear actually had not deployed, or if instead the bulb in the signal light was defective.

When the flight engineer tried to remove the light bulb, it wouldn't budge, and the other members of the crew tried to help him. As they struggled with the bulb, no one noticed the aircraft was losing altitude, and the plane simply flew right into the swamp. Dozens of people were killed in the crash. While an experienced crew of high-priced pilots fiddled with a seventy-five cent light bulb, the plane with its passengers flew right into the ground.

TIME DEADLINES AND EMERGENCIES
FORCE US TO PRIORITIZE

We find this in Parkinson's Law: If you have only one letter to write, it will take all day to do it. If you have twenty letters to write, you'll get them done in one day. When is our most efficient time in our work? The week before vacation! Why can't we always run our lives the way we do the week before we leave the office, making decisions, cleaning off the desk, returning calls? Under normal conditions, we are efficient (doing things right). When time pressure mounts or emergencies arise, we become effective (doing the right things). Efficiency is the foundation for survival. Effectiveness is the foundation of success.

On the night of April 14, 1912, the great ocean liner, the *Titanic*, crashed into an iceberg in the Atlantic and sank, causing great loss of life. One of the most curious stories to come from the disaster was of a woman who had a place in one of the lifeboats.

She asked if she could return to her stateroom for something and was given just three minutes. In her stateroom she ignored her own jewelry, and instead grabbed three oranges. Then she quickly returned to her place in the boat.

Just hours earlier it would have been ludicrous to think she would have accepted a crate of oranges in exchange for even one small diamond, but circumstances had suddenly transformed all the values aboard the ship. The emergency had clarified her priorities.

Too Often We Learn Too Late
What Is Really Important

Gary Redding tells this story about Senator Paul Tsongas of Massachusetts. In January 1984 he announced that he would retire from the U.S. Senate and not seek reelection. Tsongas was a rising political star. He was a strong favorite to be reelected, and had even been mentioned as a potential future candidate for the Presidency or Vice Presidency of the United States.

A few weeks before his announcement, Tsongas had learned he had a form of lymphatic cancer which could not be cured but could be treated. In all likelihood, it would not greatly affect his physical abilities or life expectancy. The illness did not force Tsongas out of the Senate, but it did force him to face the reality of his own mortality. He would not be able to do everything he might want to do. So what were the things he really wanted to do in the time he had?

He decided that what he wanted most in life, what he would not give up if he could not have everything, was being with his family and watching his children grow up. He would rather do that than shape the nation's laws or get his name in the history books.

Shortly after his decision was announced, a friend wrote a note to congratulate Tsongas on having his priorities straight. The note read: "Nobody on his deathbed ever said, 'I wish I had spent more time on my business.'"

5

How Do I Develop Trust?

Trust is the foundation of leadership.

One of the most important lessons a leader can learn is how trust works. To me, it is a little like earning and spending pocket change. Each time you make a good leadership decision, it puts change into your pocket. Each time you make a poor one, you have to pay out some of your change to the people.

Every leader has a certain amount of change in his pocket when he starts in a new leadership position. From then on, he either builds up his change or pays it out. If he makes one bad decision after another, he keeps paying out change. Then one day, after making one last bad decision, he is going to reach into his pocket and realize he is out of change. It doesn't even matter if the blunder was big or small. When you're out of change, you're out as a leader.

A leader's history of successes and failures makes a big difference in his credibility. Your people know when you make mistakes. The real question is whether you're going to 'fess up. If you do, you can often quickly regain their trust. I've learned firsthand that when it comes to leadership, you just can't take shortcuts, no matter how long you've been leading your people.

TRUST IS THE FOUNDATION OF LEADERSHIP

There are three qualities a leader must exemplify to build trust: competence, connection, and character. People will forgive occasional mistakes based on ability, especially if they can see that you're still growing as a leader. But they won't trust someone who has slips in character. In that area, even occasional lapses are lethal. All effective leaders know this truth. PepsiCo chairman and CEO Craig Weatherup acknowledges, "People will tolerate honest mistakes, but if you violate their trust you will find it very difficult to ever regain their confidence. That is one reason that you need to treat trust as your most precious asset. You may fool your boss but you can never fool your colleagues or subordinates."

General H. Norman Schwarzkopf points to the significance of character: "Leadership is a potent combination of strategy and character. But if you must be without one, be without strategy." Character and leadership credibility always go hand in hand. Anthony Harrigan, president of the U.S. Business and Industrial Council, said,

> The role of character always has been the key factor in the rise and fall of nations. And one can be sure that America is no exception to this rule of history. We won't survive as a country because we are smarter or more sophisticated but because we are—we hope—stronger inwardly. In short, character is the only effective bulwark against internal and external forces that lead to a country's disintegration or collapse.

Character makes trust possible. And trust makes leadership possible.

CHARACTER COMMUNICATES

Character communicates many things to followers:

CHARACTER COMMUNICATES CONSISTENCY

Leaders without inner strength can't be counted on day after day because their ability to perform changes constantly. NBA great Jerry West commented, "You can't get too much done in life if you only work on the days when you feel good." If your people don't know what to expect from you as a leader, at some point they won't look to you for leadership.

> WHEN A LEADER'S CHARACTER IS STRONG, PEOPLE
> TRUST HIM, AND THEY TRUST IN HIS ABILITY
> TO RELEASE THEIR POTENTIAL.

Think about what happened in the late 1980s. Several high-profile Christian leaders stumbled and fell due to moral issues. That lack of consistency compromised their ability to lead their people. In fact, it gave a black eye to every pastor across the nation because it caused people to become suspicious of all church leaders, regardless of their personal track records. The flawed character of those fallen leaders destroyed the foundation for their leadership.

When I think of leaders who epitomize consistency of character, the first person who comes to mind is Billy Graham. Regardless of personal religious beliefs, everybody trusts him. Why? Because he has modeled high character for more than half a century. He lives out his values every day. He never makes a commitment unless he is going to keep it. And he goes out of his way to personify integrity.

CHARACTER COMMUNICATES POTENTIAL

John Morley observed, "No man can climb out beyond the limitations of his own character." That's especially true when it comes to leadership. Take, for instance, the case of NHL coach Mike Keenan. As of mid-1997, he had a noteworthy record of professional hockey victories: the fifth greatest number of regular-season wins, the third greatest number of play-off victories, six division titles, four NHL finals appearances, and one Stanley Cup.

Yet despite those commendable credentials, Keenan was unable to stay with a single team for any length of time. In eleven and a half seasons, he coached four different teams. And after his stint with the fourth team—the St. Louis Blues—he was unable to land a job for a long time. Why? Sportswriter E. M. Swift said of Keenan, "The reluctance to hire Keenan is *easily* explicable. Everywhere he has been, he has alienated players and management."[1] Evidently, his players didn't trust him. Neither did the owners, who were benefiting from seeing their teams win.

Craig Weatherup explains, "You don't build trust by talking about it. You build it by achieving results, always with integrity and in a manner that shows real personal regard for the people with whom you work."[2] When a leader's character is strong, people trust him, and they trust in his ability to release their potential. That not only gives followers hope for the future, but it also promotes a strong belief in themselves and their organization.

CHARACTER COMMUNICATES RESPECT

When you don't have strength within, you can't earn respect without. And respect is absolutely essential for lasting leadership. How do leaders earn respect? By making sound decisions, admitting their mistakes, and putting what's best for their followers and the organization ahead of their personal agendas.

A leader's good character builds trust among his followers. But when a leader breaks trust, he forfeits his ability to lead. I was again reminded of this while listening to a lesson taught by my friend Bill Hybels. Four times a year, he and I teach a seminar called "Leading and Communicating to Change Lives." Bill was conducting a session titled "Lessons from a Leadership Nightmare," and he shared observations and insights on some of the leadership mistakes made by Robert McNamara and the Johnson administration during the Vietnam War: the administration's inability to prioritize multiple challenges, its acceptance of faulty assumptions, and Johnson's failure to face serious staff conflicts. But in my opinion, the greatest insight Bill shared during that talk concerned the failure of American leaders, including McNamara, to face and publicly admit the terrible mistakes they had made concerning the war in Vietnam. Their actions broke trust with the American people, and the United States has been suffering from the repercussions ever since.

No leader can break trust with his people and expect to keep the same level of influence with them. Trust is the foundation of leadership. Violate your people's trust, and you're through as a leader.

How Can I Effectively Cast Vision?

You can seize only what you can see.

One of the great dreamers of the twentieth century was Walt Disney. Any person who could create the first sound cartoon, first all-color cartoon, and first animated feature-length motion picture is definitely someone with vision. But Disney's greatest masterpieces of vision were Disneyland and Walt Disney World. And the spark for that vision came from an unexpected place.

Back when Walt's two daughters were young, he took them to an amusement park in the Los Angeles area on Saturday mornings. His girls loved it, and he did too. An amusement park is a kid's paradise, with wonderful atmosphere.

Walt was especially captivated by the carousel. As he approached it, he saw a blur of bright images racing around to the tune of energetic calliope music. But when he got closer and the carousel stopped, he could see that his eye had been fooled. He observed shabby horses with cracked and chipped paint. And he noticed that only the horses on the outside row moved up and down. The others stood lifeless, bolted to the floor.

The cartoonist's disappointment inspired him with a grand vision. In his mind's eye he could see an amusement park where the illusion didn't evaporate, where children and adults could enjoy a carnival atmosphere without the seedy side that accompanies some circuses or traveling carnivals. His dream became Disneyland. As Larry Taylor stated in *Be an Orange*, Walt's vision could be summarized as, "No chipped paint. All the horses jump."

Look Before You Lead

Vision is everything for a leader. It is utterly indispensable. Why? Because vision leads the leader. It paints the target. It sparks and fuels the fire within, and draws him forward. It is also the fire lighter for others who follow that leader. Show me a leader without vision, and I'll show you someone who isn't going anywhere. At best, he is traveling in circles.

To get a handle on vision and how it comes to be a part of a good leader's life, understand these things:

Vision Starts Within

When I'm teaching at conferences, someone will occasionally ask me to give him a vision for his organization.

But I can't do it. You can't buy, beg, or borrow vision. It has to come from the inside. For Disney, vision was never a problem. Because of his creativity and desire for excellence, he always saw what *could* be.

If you lack vision, look inside yourself. Draw on your natural gifts and desires. Look to your calling if you have one. And if you still don't sense a vision of your own, then consider hooking up with a leader whose vision resonates with you. Become his partner. That's what Walt Disney's brother, Roy, did. He was a good businessman and leader who could make things happen, but Walt provided the vision. Together, they made an incredible team.

VISION DRAWS ON YOUR HISTORY

Vision isn't some mystical quality that comes out of a vacuum, as some people seem to believe. It grows from a leader's past and the history of the people around him. That was the case for Disney. But it's true for all leaders. Talk to any leader, and you're likely to discover key events in his past that were instrumental in the creation of his vision.

VISION MEETS OTHERS' NEEDS

True vision is far-reaching. It goes beyond what one individual can accomplish. And if it has real value, it does more than just *include* others; it *adds value* to them. If you have a vision that doesn't serve others, it's probably too small.

VISION HELPS YOU GATHER RESOURCES

One of the most valuable benefits of vision is that it acts like a magnet—attracting, challenging, and uniting people. It also rallies finances and other resources. The greater the vision, the more winners it has the potential to attract. The more challenging the vision, the harder the participants fight to achieve it. Edwin Land, the founder of Polaroid, advised, "The first thing you do is teach the person to feel that the vision is very important and nearly impossible. That draws out the drive in winners."

FOCUS ON LISTENING

Where does vision come from? To find the vision that is indispensable to leadership, you have to become a good listener. You must listen to several voices.

THE INNER VOICE

As I have already said, vision starts within. Do you know your life's mission? What stirs your heart? What do you dream about? If what you're pursuing doesn't come from a desire within—from the very depths of who you are and what you believe—you will not be able to accomplish it.

THE UNHAPPY VOICE

Where does inspiration for great ideas come from? From noticing what *doesn't* work. Discontent with the *status quo* is a great catalyst for vision. Are you on complacent cruise control? Or do you find yourself itching to change your world? No great leader in history has fought to prevent change.

THE SUCCESSFUL VOICE

Nobody can accomplish great things alone. To fulfill a big vision, you need a good team. But you also need good advice from someone who is ahead of you in the leadership journey. If you want to lead others to greatness, find a mentor. Do you have an adviser who can help you sharpen your vision?

THINK ABOUT WHAT YOU'D LIKE TO SEE CHANGE
IN THE WORLD AROUND YOU.

THE HIGHER VOICE

Although it's true that your vision must come from within, you shouldn't let it be confined by your limited capabilities. A truly valuable vision must have God in it. Only He knows your full capabilities. Have you looked beyond yourself, even beyond your own lifetime, as you've sought your vision? If not, you may be missing your true potential and life's best for you.

To improve your vision, do the following:

Measure yourself. If you have previously thought about the vision for your life and articulated it, measure how well you are carrying it out. Talk to several key people, such as your spouse, a close friend, and key employees, asking them to state what they think your vision is. If *they* can articulate it, then *you* are probably living it.

Do a gut check. If you haven't done a lot of work on vision, spend the next several weeks or months thinking about it. Consider what really impacts you at a gut level. *What makes you cry? What makes you dream? What gives you energy?*

Also think about what you'd like to see change in the world around you. What do you see that isn't—but could be? Once your ideas start to become clearer, write them down and talk to a mentor about them.

From 1923 to 1955, Robert Woodruff served as president of Coca-Cola. During that time, he wanted Coca-Cola to be available to every American serviceman around the world for five cents, no matter what it cost the company. What a bold goal! But it was nothing compared to the bigger picture he could see in his mind's eye. In his lifetime, he wanted every person in the *world* to have tasted Coca-Cola. When you look deep into your heart and soul for a vision, what do *you* see?

PART 3

THE IMPACT OF
A LEADER

7

WHY IS INFLUENCE IMPORTANT?

*The true measure of leadership is influence—
nothing more, nothing less.*

I f you don't have influence, you will *never* be able to lead
others. So how do you find and measure influence?
Here's a story to answer that question.

In late summer of 1997, people were jolted by two
events that occurred less than a week apart: the deaths of
Princess Diana and Mother Teresa. On the surface, the two
women could not have been more different. One was a tall,
young, glamorous princess from England who circulated in
the highest society. The other, a Nobel Peace Prize recipi-
ent, was a small, elderly Catholic nun born in Albania, who
served the poorest of the poor in Calcutta, India.

What's incredible is that their impact was remarkably
similar. In a 1996 poll published by the London *Daily
Mail,* Princess Diana and Mother Teresa were voted in first
and second places as the world's two most caring people.

That's something that doesn't happen unless you have a lot of influence. How did someone like Diana come to be regarded in the same way as Mother Teresa? The answer is that she demonstrated the power of influence.

DIANA CAPTURED THE WORLD'S IMAGINATION

In 1981, Diana became the most talked-about person on the globe when she married Prince Charles of England. Nearly one billion people watched Diana's wedding ceremony televised from St. Paul's Cathedral. And since that day, it seemed people never could get enough news about her. People were intrigued with Diana, a commoner who had once been a kindergarten teacher. At first she seemed painfully shy and totally overwhelmed by all the attention she and her new husband were receiving. Early in their marriage, some reports stated that Diana wasn't very happy performing the duties expected of her as a royal princess. However, in time she adjusted to her new role. As she started traveling and representing the royal family around the world at various functions, she quickly made it her goal to serve others and raise funds for numerous charitable causes. And during the process, she built many important relationships—with politicians, organizers of humanitarian causes, entertainers, and heads of state.

Diana started rallying people to causes such as medical research for AIDS, care for people with leprosy, and a ban on land mines. She was quite influential in bringing that last issue to the attention of the world's leaders. On a visit to the United States just months before her death, she met with members of the Clinton administration to convince them to support the Oslo conference banning the devices. And a few weeks later, they made changes in their position. Patrick Fuller of the British Red Cross said, "The attention she drew to the issue influenced Clinton. She put the issue on the world agenda, there's no doubt about that."[1]

THE EMERGENCE OF A LEADER

In the beginning, Diana's title had merely given her a platform to address others, but she soon became a person of influence in her own right. In 1996 when she was divorced from Prince Charles, she lost her title, but that loss didn't at all diminish her impact on others. Instead, her influence continued to increase while that of her former husband and in-laws declined—despite their royal titles and position.

Ironically, even in death Diana continued to influence others. When her funeral was broadcast on television and BBC Radio, it was translated into forty-four languages.

NBC estimated that the total audience numbered as many as 2.5 billion people—more than twice the number of people who watched her wedding.

TRUE LEADERSHIP CANNOT BE AWARDED, APPOINTED, OR ASSIGNED. IT COMES ONLY FROM INFLUENCE.

Princess Diana has been characterized in many ways. But one word that I've never heard used to describe her is *leader*. Yet that's what she was. Ultimately, she made things happen because she was an influencer, and leadership is influence—nothing more, nothing less.

FIVE MYTHS ABOUT LEADERSHIP

There are plenty of misconceptions and myths that people embrace about leaders and leadership. Here are five common ones:

1. THE MANAGEMENT MYTH

A widespread misunderstanding is that leading and managing are one and the same. Up until a few years ago, books that claimed to be on leadership were often really about management. The main difference between the two is that leadership is about influencing people to follow, while management focuses on maintaining systems and processes. The best way to test whether a person can lead rather than just manage is to ask him to create positive change. Managers can maintain direction, but they can't change it. To move people in a new direction, you need influence.

2. THE ENTREPRENEUR MYTH

Frequently, people assume that all salespeople and entrepreneurs are leaders. But that's not always the case. You may remember the Ronco commercials that appeared on television years ago. They sold items such as the Veg-O-Matic, Pocket Fisherman, and Inside-the-Shell Egg Scrambler. Those products were the brainchildren of an entrepreneur named Ron Popeil. Called the salesman of the century, he has also appeared in numerous infomercials for products such as spray-on relief for baldness and food dehydrating devices.

Popeil is certainly enterprising, innovative, and successful, especially if you measure him by the $300 million in sales his products have earned. But that doesn't make him a leader. People may be buying what he has to sell, but they're not following him. At best, he is able to persuade people for a moment, but he holds no long-term influence with them.

3. THE KNOWLEDGE MYTH

Sir Francis Bacon said, "Knowledge is power." Most people, believing power is the essence of leadership, naturally assume that those who possess knowledge and intelligence are leaders. But that isn't automatically true. You can visit any major university and meet brilliant research scientists and philosophers whose ability to think is so high that it's off the charts, but whose ability to lead is so low that it doesn't even register on the charts. IQ doesn't necessarily equate to leadership.

4. THE PIONEER MYTH

Another misconception is that anyone who is out in front of the crowd is a leader. But being first isn't always the same as leading. For example, Sir Edmund Hillary was the first man to reach the summit of Mount Everest. Since his historic ascent in 1953, many people have "followed" him in achieving that feat. But that doesn't make Hillary a leader. He wasn't even the leader on that particular expedition. John Hunt was. And when Hillary traveled to the South Pole in 1958 as part of the Commonwealth Trans-Antarctic Expedition, he was accompanying another leader, Sir Vivian Fuchs. To be a leader, a person has to not only be out front, but also have people intentionally coming behind him, following his lead, and acting on his vision.

5. THE POSITION MYTH

The greatest misunderstanding about leadership is that people think it is based on position, but it's not. Stanley Huffty affirmed, "It's not the position that makes the leader; it's the leader that makes the position."

Look at what happened several years ago at Cordiant, the advertising agency formerly known as Saatchi & Saatchi. In 1994, institutional investors at Saatchi & Saatchi forced the board of directors to dismiss Maurice Saatchi, the company's CEO. What was the result? Several executives followed him out. So did many of the company's largest accounts, including British Airways and Mars, the candy maker. Saatchi's influence was so great that his departure caused the company's stock to fall immediately from $8⅝ to $4 per share.[2] Saatchi lost his title and position, but he continued to be the leader.

WHO'S THE REAL LEADER?

I personally learned the significance of influence when I accepted my first job out of college at a small church in rural Indiana. I went in with all the right credentials. I was hired as the senior pastor, which meant that I possessed the position and title of leader in that organization. I had the proper college degree. I had even been ordained. In addition, I had been trained by my father who was an excellent pastor and a very high-profile leader in the denomination. It made for a good-looking résumé—but it didn't make me a leader. At my first board meeting, I quickly found out who was the real leader of that church. By the time I took my next position three years later, I had learned the importance of influence. I recognized that hard work was required to gain influence in any organization and to earn the right to become the leader.

LEADERSHIP WITHOUT LEVERAGE

I admire and respect the leadership of my good friend Bill Hybels, the senior pastor of Willow Creek Community Church in South Barrington, Illinois, the largest church in North America. Bill says he believes that the church is the most leadership-intensive enterprise in society. A lot of businesspeople I know are surprised when they hear that statement, but I think Bill is right. What is the basis of his belief? Positional leadership doesn't work in volunteer organizations. If a leader doesn't have leverage—or influence—then he is ineffective. In other organizations, the person who has position has incredible leverage. In the military, leaders can use rank and, if all else fails, throw people into the brig. In business, bosses have tremendous leverage in the form of salary, benefits, and perks. Most followers are pretty cooperative when their livelihood is at stake.

FOLLOWERS IN VOLUNTARY ORGANIZATIONS
CANNOT BE FORCED TO GET ON BOARD.
IF THE LEADER HAS NO INFLUENCE WITH
THEM, THEN THEY WON'T FOLLOW.

But in voluntary organizations, such as churches, the only thing that works is leadership in its purest form. Leaders have only their influence to aid them. And as Harry A. Overstreet observed, "The very essence of all power to influence lies in getting the other person to participate." Followers in voluntary organizations cannot be forced to get on board. If the leader has no influence with them, then they won't follow. If you are a businessperson and you really want to find out whether your people are capable of leading, send them out to volunteer their time in the community. If they can get people to follow them while they're serving at the Red Cross, a United Way shelter, or their local church, then you know that they really do have influence—and leadership ability.

Here is my favorite leadership proverb: "He who thinks he leads, but has no followers, is only taking a walk." If you can't influence others, they won't follow you. And if they won't follow, you're not a leader. No matter what anybody else tells you, remember that leadership is influence—nothing more, nothing less.

8

How Does Influence Work?

*Real leadership is being the person others
will gladly and confidently follow.*

Sociologists tell us that even the most introverted individual influences ten thousand other people during his or her lifetime! This amazing statistic was shared with me by my associate Tim Elmore. Tim and I concluded that each one of us is both influencing and being influenced by others.

Influence Can Be Developed

The prominent leader of any group is quite easily discovered. Just observe the people as they gather. If an issue is to be decided, who is the person whose opinion seems most valuable? Who is the one with whom people quickly agree? Most importantly, who is the one the others follow?

Robert Dilenschneider, the CEO of Hill and Knowlton, a worldwide public relations agency, is one of the nation's major influence brokers. He skillfully weaves his persuasive magic in the global arena where governments and mega-corporations meet. He wrote a book entitled *Power and Influence*, in which he shares the idea of the "power triangle" to help leaders get ahead. He says, "The three components of this triangle are communication, recognition, and influence. You start to communicate effectively. This leads to recognition and recognition in turn leads to influence."[1]

THE LEVELS OF LEADERSHIP

We can increase our influence and leadership potential if we understand the following levels of leadership:

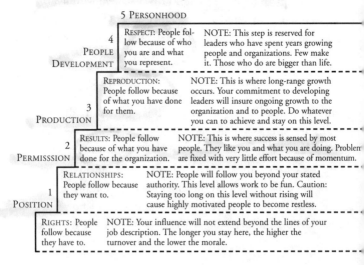

5 PERSONHOOD

| 4 PEOPLE DEVELOPMENT | RESPECT: People follow because of who you are and what you represent. | NOTE: This step is reserved for leaders who have spent years growing people and organizations. Few make it. Those who do are bigger than life. |

| 3 PRODUCTION | REPRODUCTION: People follow because of what you have done for them. | NOTE: This is where long-range growth occurs. Your commitment to developing leaders will insure ongoing growth to the organization and to people. Do whatever you can to achieve and stay on this level. |

| 2 PERMISSSION | RESULTS: People follow because of what you have done for the organization. | NOTE: This is where success is sensed by most people. They like you and what you are doing. Problems are fixed with very little effort because of momentum. |

| 1 POSITION | RELATIONSHIPS: People follow because they want to. | NOTE: People will follow you beyond your stated authority. This level allows work to be fun. Caution: Staying too long on this level without rising will cause highly motivated people to become restless. |

| | RIGHTS: People follow because they have to. | NOTE: Your influence will not extend beyond the lines of your job description. The longer you stay here, the higher the turnover and the lower the morale. |

LEVEL 1: POSITION—PEOPLE FOLLOW
BECAUSE THEY HAVE TO

This is the basic entry level of leadership. The only influence you have is that which comes with a title. People who stay at this level get into territorial rights, protocol, tradition, and organizational charts. These things are not negative unless they become the basis for authority and influence, but they are poor substitutes for leadership skills.

A person may be "in control" because he has been appointed to a position. In that position he may have authority. But real leadership is more than having authority; it is more than having the technical training and following the proper procedures. Real leadership is being the person others will gladly and confidently follow. A real leader knows the difference between being the boss and being a leader.

- The boss drives his workers; the leader coaches them.
- The boss depends upon authority; the leader on goodwill.
- The boss inspires fear; the leader inspires enthusiasm.
- The boss says "I"; the leader, "we."
- The boss fixes the blame for the breakdown; the leader fixes the breakdown.

Characteristics of a "Positional Leader"

Security is based on title, not talent. The story is told of a private in World War I who shouted on the battlefield, "Put out that match!" only to find to his chagrin that the offender was General "Black Jack" Pershing. When the private, who feared severe punishment, tried to stammer out his apology, General Pershing patted him on the back and said, "That's all right, son. Just be glad I'm not a second lieutenant." The point should be clear. The higher the person's level of true ability and the resulting influence, the more secure and confident he becomes.

This level is often gained by appointment. All other levels are gained by ability. Leo Durocher was coaching at first base in an exhibition game the Giants were playing at West Point. One noisy cadet kept shouting at Leo and doing his best to upset him.

"Hey, Durocher," he hollered. "How did a little squirt like you get into the major leagues?"

Leo shouted back, "My congressman appointed me!"[2]

People will not follow a positional leader beyond his stated authority. They will only do what they have to do when they are required to do it. Low morale is always present. When the leader lacks confidence, the followers lack commitment. They are like the little boy who was asked by Billy Graham how to find the nearest post office. When the lad told him, Dr. Graham thanked him and said, "If you'll come to the convention center this evening you can hear me telling everyone how to get to heaven."

"I don't think I'll be there," the boy replied. "You don't even know your way to the post office."

Positional leaders have more difficulty working with volunteers, white collar workers, and younger people. Volunteers don't have to work in the organization so there is no monetary leverage that a positional leader can use to make them respond. White collar workers are used to participating in decision-making and resent dictatorial leadership. Baby boomers in particular are unimpressed with symbols of authority.

The following characteristics must be exhibited with excellence on this level before you can advance to the next level.

Level 1: Position/Rights

- Know your job description thoroughly.
- Be aware of the history of the organization.
- Relate the organization's history to the people of the organization (in other words, be a team player).
- Accept responsibility.
- Do your job with consistent excellence.
- Do more than expected.
- Offer creative ideas for change and improvement.

LEVEL 2: PERMISSION—PEOPLE FOLLOW
BECAUSE THEY WANT TO

Fred Smith says, "Leadership is getting people to work for you when they are not obligated."[3] That will only happen when you climb to the second level of influence. People don't care how much you know until they know how much you care. Leadership begins with the heart, not the head. It flourishes with a meaningful relationship, not more regulations.

A person on the "permission" level will lead by interrelationships. The agenda is not the pecking order but people development. On this level, the leader donates time, energy, and focus on the follower's needs and desires. A wonderful illustration of why it's so critical to put people and their needs first is found in the story of Henry Ford in Amitai Etzioni's book, *Modern Organizations*: "He made a perfect car, the Model T, that ended the need for any other car. He was totally product-oriented. He wanted to fill the world with Model T cars. But when people started coming to him and saying, 'Mr. Ford, we'd like a different color car,' he remarked, 'You can have any color you want as long as it's black.' And that's when the decline started."

People who are unable to build solid, lasting relationships will soon discover that they are unable to sustain long, effective leadership. Needless to say, you can love people without leading them, but you cannot lead people without loving them.

Caution! Don't try to skip a level. The most often skipped level is 2, *Permission*. For example, a husband goes from level 1, *Position*, a wedding day title, to level 3, *Production*. He becomes a great provider for the family, but in the process he neglects the essential relationships that hold a family together. The family disintegrates and so does the husband's business. Relationships involve a process that provides the glue and much of the staying power for long-term, consistent production.

The following characteristics must be mastered on this level before you can advance to the next one.

Level 2: Permission/Relationship

- Possess a genuine love for people.
- Make those who work with you more successful.
- See through other people's eyes.
- Love people more than procedures.
- Do "win-win" or don't do it.
- Include others in your journey.
- Deal wisely with difficult people.

LEVEL 3: PRODUCTION—PEOPLE FOLLOW BECAUSE
OF WHAT YOU HAVE DONE FOR THE ORGANIZATION

On this level things begin to happen, good things. Profit

increases. Morale is high. Turnover is low. Needs are being met. Goals are being realized. Accompanying the growth is the "big mo"—momentum. Leading and influencing others is fun. Problems are solved with minimum effort. Fresh statistics are shared on a regular basis with the people who undergird the growth of the organization. Everyone is results-oriented. In fact, results are the main reason for the activity.

This is a major difference between levels 2 and 3. On the "relationship" level, people get together just to get together. There is no other objective. On the "results" level, people come together to accomplish a purpose. They like to get together to get together, but they love to get together to accomplish something. In other words, they are results-oriented.

The following characteristics must be mastered with excellence before you can advance to the next level.

Level 3: Production/Results

- Initiate and accept responsibility for growth.
- Develop and follow a statement of purpose.
- Make your job description and energy an integral part of the statement of purpose.
- Develop accountability for results, beginning with yourself.
- Know and do the things that give a high return.

- Communicate the strategy and vision of the organization.
- Become a change-agent and understand timing.
- Make the difficult decisions that will make a difference.

LEVEL 4: PEOPLE DEVELOPMENT—PEOPLE FOLLOW BECAUSE OF WHAT YOU HAVE DONE FOR THEM

A leader is great, not because of his or her power, but because of his or her ability to empower others. Success without a successor is failure. A worker's main responsibility is doing the work himself. A leader's responsibility is developing others to do the work. The true leader can be recognized because somehow his people consistently demonstrate superior performances.

Loyalty to the leader reaches its highest peak when the follower has personally grown through the mentorship of the leader. Note the progression: At level 2, the follower loves the leader; at level 3, the follower admires the leader; at level 4, the follower is loyal to the leader. Why? You win people's hearts by helping them grow personally.

The core of leaders who surround you should all be people you have personally touched or helped to develop in some way. When that happens, love and loyalty will be exhibited by those closest to you and by those who are touched by your key leaders.

There is, however, a potential problem of moving up the levels of influence as a leader and becoming comfortable with the group of people you have developed around you. Many new people may view you as a "position" leader because you have had no contact with them. These two suggestions will help you become a people developer:

1. Walk slowly through the crowd. Have some way of keeping in touch with everyone.

2. Develop key leaders. I systematically meet with and teach those who are influencers within the organization. They in turn pass on to others what I have given them.

The characteristics that must be mastered at this level are listed below.

Level 4: People Development/Reproduction

- Realize that people are your most valuable asset.
- Place a priority on developing people.
- Be a model for others to follow.
- Pour your leadership efforts into the top 20 percent of your people.
- Expose key leaders to growth opportunities.
- Attract other winners/producers to the common goal.
- Surround yourself with an inner core that complements your leadership.

LEVEL 5: PERSONHOOD—PEOPLE FOLLOW BECAUSE OF WHO YOU ARE AND WHAT YOU REPRESENT

Most of us have not yet arrived at this level. Only a lifetime of proven leadership will allow us to sit at level 5 and reap the rewards that are eternally satisfying. I do know this—some day I want to sit atop this level. It's achievable.

The following characteristics define the Level 5 leader.

Level 5: Personhood/Respect

- Your followers are loyal and sacrificial.
- You have spent years mentoring and molding leaders.
- You have become a statesman/consultant, and are sought out by others.
- Your greatest joy comes from watching others grow and develop.
- You transcend the organization.

CLIMBING THE STEPS OF LEADERSHIP

Here are some additional insights on the leadership-levels process:

THE HIGHER YOU GO, THE LONGER IT TAKES.

Each time there is a change in your job or you join a new circle of friends, you start on the lowest level and begin to work yourself up the steps.

THE HIGHER YOU GO, THE HIGHER THE LEVEL
OF COMMITMENT.

This increase in commitment is a two-way street. Greater commitment is demanded not only from you, but from the other individuals involved. When either the leader or the follower is unwilling to make the sacrifices a new level demands, influence will begin to decrease.

THE HIGHER YOU GO, THE EASIER IT IS TO LEAD.

Notice the progression from level two through level four. The focus goes from liking you to liking what you do for the common interest of all concerned (to liking what you do for them personally). Each level climbed by the leader and the followers adds another reason why people will want to follow.

THE HIGHER YOU GO, THE GREATER THE GROWTH.

Growth can only occur when effective change takes place. Change will become easier as you climb the levels of leadership. As you rise, other people will allow and even assist you in making the needed changes.

YOU NEVER LEAVE THE BASE LEVEL.

Each level stands upon the previous one and will crumble if the lower level is neglected. For example, if you move from a permission (relationships) level to a production (results) level and stop caring for the people who are following you and helping you produce, they might begin to develop a feeling of being used. As you move up in the levels, the deeper and more solid your leadership will be with a person or group of people.

IF YOU ARE LEADING A GROUP OF PEOPLE, YOU WILL NOT BE ON THE SAME LEVEL WITH EVERYONE.

Not every person will respond the same way to your leadership.

FOR YOUR LEADERSHIP TO REMAIN EFFECTIVE, IT IS ESSENTIAL THAT YOU TAKE THE OTHER INFLUENCERS WITHIN THE GROUP WITH YOU TO THE HIGHER LEVELS.

The collective influence of you and the other leaders will bring the rest along. If this does not happen, divided interest and loyalty will occur within the group.

YOU MUST KNOW WHAT LEVEL YOU ARE ON AT THIS MOMENT.

Since you will be on different levels with different people, you need to know which people are on which level. If the biggest influencers within the organization are on the highest levels and are supportive of you, then your success in leading others will be attainable. If the best influencers are on the highest levels and not supportive, then problems will soon arise.

Everyone is a leader because everyone influences someone. Not everyone will become a great leader, but everyone can become a better leader. Are you willing to unleash your leadership potential? Will you use your leadership skills to better mankind?

My Influence

My life shall touch a dozen lives
Before this day is done.
Leave countless marks of good or ill,
E'er sets the evening sun.

This, the wish I always wish,
The prayer I always pray:
Lord, may my life help other lives
It touches by the way.[4]

9

HOW CAN I EXTEND MY INFLUENCE?

The act of empowering others changes lives.

An English artist named William Wolcott went to New York in 1924 to record his impressions of that fascinating city. One morning he was visiting in the office of a former colleague when the urge to sketch came over him. Seeing some paper on his friend's desk, he asked, "May I have that?"

His friend answered, "That's not sketching paper. That's ordinary wrapping paper."

Not wanting to lose that spark of inspiration, Wolcott took the wrapping paper and said, "Nothing is ordinary if you know how to use it." On that ordinary paper Wolcott made two sketches. Later that same year, one of those same sketches sold for $500 and the other for $1,000, quite a sum for 1924.

People under the influence of an empowering person are like paper in the hands of a talented artist. No matter what they're made of, they can become treasures.

The ability to empower others is one of the keys to personal and professional success. John Craig remarked, "No matter how much work you can do, no matter how engaging your personality may be, you will not advance far in business if you cannot work through others." And business executive J. Paul Getty asserted, "It doesn't make much difference how much other knowledge or experience an executive possesses; if he is unable to achieve results through people, he is worthless as an executive."

PEOPLE UNDER THE INFLUENCE OF AN
EMPOWERING PERSON ARE LIKE PAPER IN THE HANDS
OF A TALENTED ARTIST.

When you become an empowerer, you work with and through people, but you do much more. You enable others to reach the highest levels in their personal and professional development. Simply defined, empowering is giving your influence to others for the purpose of personal and organizational growth. It's sharing yourself—your influence, position, power, and opportunities—with others for the purpose of investing in their lives so that they can function at their best. It's seeing people's potential, sharing your resources with them, and showing them that you believe in them completely.

You may already be empowering some people in your

life without knowing it. When you entrust your spouse with an important decision and then cheerfully back him up, that's empowering. When you decide that your child is ready to cross the street by herself and give her your permission to do so, you have empowered her. When you delegate a challenging job to an employee and give her the authority she needs to get it done, you have empowered her.

The act of empowering others changes lives, and it's a win-win situation for you and the people you empower. Giving others your authority isn't like giving away an object, such as your car, for example. If you give away your car, you're stuck. You no longer have transportation. But empowering others by giving them your authority has the same effect as sharing information: You haven't lost anything. You have increased the ability of others without decreasing yourself.

QUALIFICATIONS OF AN EMPOWERER

Just about everyone has the potential to become an empowerer, but you cannot empower everyone. The process works only when certain conditions are met. You must have:

POSITION

You cannot empower people whom you don't lead. Leadership expert Fred Smith explained, "Who can give permission for another person to succeed? A person in authority. Others can encourage, but permission comes only from an authority figure: a parent, boss, or pastor."

RELATIONSHIP

It has been said that relationships are forged, not formed. They require time and common experience. If you have made the effort to connect with people, then by the time you're ready to empower them, your relationship should be solid enough for you to be able to lead them. And as you do, remember what Ralph Waldo Emerson wrote, "Every man [or woman] is entitled to be valued by his [or her] best moments." When you value people and your relationships with them, you lay the foundation for empowering others.

RESPECT

Relationships cause people to want to be with you, but respect causes them to want to be empowered by you. Mutual respect is essential to the empowerment process. Psychiatrist Ari Kiev summed it up this way: "Everyone wants to feel that he counts for something and is important to someone. Invariably, people will give their love, respect, and attention to the person who fills that need." When you believe in people, care about them, and trust them, they know it. And that respect inspires them to want to follow where you lead.

COMMITMENT

The last quality a leader needs to become an empowerer is commitment. US Air executive Ed McElroy stressed that "commitment gives us new power. No matter what comes to us—sickness, poverty, or disaster, we never turn our eye from the goal." The process of empowering others isn't always easy, especially when you start doing it for the first time. It's a road that has many bumps and sidetracks. But it is one that's worth traveling because the rewards are so great. Remember: when you empower people, you're not influencing just them; you're influencing all the people they influence. That's impact!

THE RIGHT ATTITUDE

One more crucial element of empowering needs to be in place if you want to become a successful leader: You need to have the right attitude.

Many people neglect to empower others because they are insecure. They are afraid of losing their jobs to the people they mentor. They don't want to be replaced or displaced, even if it means that they would be able to move up to a higher position and leave their current one to be filled by the person they mentor. They're afraid of change. But change is part of empowerment—for the people you empower and for yourself. If you want to go up, there are things you have to be willing to give up.

WHEN IT COMES DOWN TO IT, EMPOWERING LEADERSHIP IS SOMETIMES THE ONLY REAL ADVANTAGE ONE ORGANIZATION HAS OVER ANOTHER IN OUR COMPETITIVE SOCIETY.

If you're not sure about where you stand in terms of your attitude toward the changes involved with empowering others, answer these questions:

QUESTIONS TO ASK BEFORE YOU GET STARTED
1. Do I believe in people and feel that they are my organization's most appreciable asset?
2. Do I believe that empowering others can accomplish more than individual achievement?
3. Do I actively search for potential leaders to empower?
4. Would I be willing to raise others to a level higher than my own level of leadership?
5. Would I be willing to invest time developing people who have leadership potential?
6. Would I be willing to let others get credit for what I taught them?
7. Do I allow others freedom of personality and process, or do I have to be in control?

8. Would I be willing to publicly give my authority and influence to potential leaders?

9. Would I be willing to let others work me out of a job?

10. Would I be willing to hand the leadership baton to the people I empower and truly root for them?

If you answer no to more than a couple of these questions, you may need an attitude adjustment. You need to believe in others enough to give them all you can and in yourself enough to know that it won't hurt you. Just remember that as long as you continue to grow and develop yourself, you'll always have something to give, and you won't need to worry about being displaced.

How to Empower Others to Their Potential

Once you have confidence in yourself and in the persons you wish to empower, you're ready to start the process. Your goal should be to hand over relatively small, simple tasks in the beginning and progressively increase their responsibilities and authority. The greener the people you're working with, the more time the process will take. But no matter whether they are raw recruits or seasoned veterans, it's still important to take them through the whole process. Use the following steps to guide you as you empower others:

1. EVALUATE THEM

The place to start when empowering people is to evaluate them. If you give inexperienced people too much authority too soon, you can set them up to fail. If you move too slowly with people who have lots of experience, you can frustrate and demoralize them.

Remember that all people have the potential to succeed. Your job is to see the potential, find out what they lack to develop it, and equip them with what they need. As you evaluate the people you intend to empower, look at these areas:

Knowledge. Think about what people need to know in order to do any task you intend to give them. Don't take for granted that they know all that you know. Ask them questions. Give them history or background information. Cast a vision by giving them the big picture of how their actions fit into the organization's mission and goals. Knowledge is not only power; it's empowering.

Skill. Examine the skill level of the people you desire to empower. Nothing is more frustrating than being asked to do things for which you have no ability. Your job as the empowerer is to find out what the job requires and make sure your people have what they need to succeed.

Desire. Greek philosopher Plutarch remarked, "The richest soil, if uncultivated, produces the rankest weeds." No amount of skill, knowledge, or potential can help people succeed if they don't have the desire to be successful. But when desire is present, empowerment is easy. As seventeenth-century French essayist Jean La Fontaine wrote, "Man is made so that whenever anything fires his soul, impossibilities vanish."

2. MODEL FOR THEM

Even people with knowledge, skill, and desire need to know what's expected of them, and the best way to inform them is to show them. People do what people see.

The people you desire to empower need to see what it looks like to fly. As their mentor, you have the best opportunity to show them. Model the attitude and work ethic you would like them to embrace. And anytime you can include them in your work, take them along with you. There is no better way to help them learn and understand what you want them to do.

3. GIVE THEM PERMISSION TO SUCCEED

As a leader and influencer, you may believe that everyone wants to be successful and automatically strives for success, probably as you have. But not everyone you influence will think the same way you do. You have to help others believe that they can succeed and show them that you want them to succeed. How do you do that?

Expect it. Author and professional speaker Danny Cox advised, "The important thing to remember is that if you don't have that inspired enthusiasm that is contagious—whatever you do have is also contagious." People can sense your underlying attitude no matter what you say or do. If you have an expectation for your people to be successful, they will know it.

Verbalize it. People need to hear you tell them that you believe in them and want them to succeed. Tell them often that you know they are going to make it. Send them encouraging notes. Become a positive prophet of their success. And reinforce your thoughts as often as you can.

Once people recognize and understand that you genuinely want to see them succeed and are committed to helping them, they will begin to believe they can accomplish what you give them to do.

4. TRANSFER AUTHORITY TO THEM

Many people are willing to give others responsibility. They gladly delegate tasks to them. But empowering others is more than sharing your workload. It's sharing your power and ability to get things done.

Management expert Peter Drucker asserted, "No executive has ever suffered because his subordinates were strong and effective." People become strong and effective only when they are given the opportunity to make decisions, initiate actions, solve problems, and meet challenges. When it comes down to it, empowering leadership is sometimes the only real advantage one organization has over another in our competitive society.

5. Publicly Show Your Confidence in Them

When you first transfer authority to the people you empower, you need to tell them that you believe in them, and you need to do it publicly. Public recognition lets them know that you believe they will succeed. But it also lets the other people they're working with know that they have your support and that your authority backs them up. It's a tangible way of sharing (and spreading) your influence.

As you raise up leaders, show them and their followers that they have your confidence and authority. And you will find that they quickly become empowered to succeed.

6. Supply Them with Feedback

Although you need to publicly praise your people, you can't let them go very long without giving them honest, positive feedback. Meet with them privately to coach them through their mistakes, miscues, and misjudgments. At first, some people may have a difficult time. During that early period, be a grace giver. Try to give them what they need, not what they deserve. And applaud any progress that they make. People do what gets praised.

7. RELEASE THEM TO CONTINUE ON THEIR OWN

No matter who you are working to empower—your employees, children, colleagues, or spouse—your ultimate aim should be to release them to make good decisions and succeed on their own. And that means giving them as much freedom as possible as soon as they are ready for it.

President Abraham Lincoln was a master at empowering his leaders. For example, when he appointed General Ulysses S. Grant as commander of the Union armies in 1864, he sent him this message: "I neither ask nor desire to know anything of your plans. Take the responsibility and act, and call on me for assistance."

That's the attitude you need as an empowerer. Give authority and responsibility, and offer assistance as needed. The person who has been the most empowering in my life is my father, Melvin Maxwell. He always encouraged me to be the best person I could be, and he gave me his permission and his power whenever he could. Years later when we talked about it, my father told me his philosophy: "I never consciously limited you as long as I knew what you were doing was morally right." Now that's an empowering attitude!

The Results of Empowerment

If you head up any kind of organization—a business, club, church, or family—learning to empower others is one of the most important things you'll ever do as its leader. Empowerment has an incredibly high return. It not only helps the individuals you raise up by making them more confident, energetic, and productive, but it also has the ability to improve your life, give you additional freedom, and promote the growth and health of your organization.

As you empower others, you will find that most aspects of your life will change for the better. Empowering others can free you personally to have more time for the important things in your life, increase the effectiveness of your organization, increase your influence with others and, best of all, make an incredibly positive impact on the lives of the people you empower.

10

How Can I Make My Leadership Last?

A leader's lasting value is measured by succession.

In 1997, one of the finest business leaders in the world died. His name was Roberto Goizueta, and he was the chairman and chief executive of the Coca-Cola Company. In a speech he gave to the Executives' Club of Chicago a few months before he died, Goizueta made this statement: "A billion hours ago, human life appeared on Earth. A billion minutes ago, Christianity emerged. A billion seconds ago, the Beatles performed on 'The Ed Sullivan Show.' A billion Coca-Colas ago . . . was yesterday morning. And the question we are asking ourselves now is, 'What must we do to make a billion Coca-Colas ago this morning?'"

Making Coca-Cola the best company in the world was Goizueta's lifelong quest, one he was still pursuing diligently when he suddenly, unexpectedly died. Companies that lose a CEO often go into turmoil, especially if his departure is unexpected, as Goizueta's was. Shortly before his death, Goizueta said in an interview with the *Atlanta Journal-Constitution* that retirement was "not on my radar screen. As long as I'm having the fun I'm having, as long as I have the energy necessary, as long as I'm not keeping people from their day in the sun, and as long as the board wants me to stay on, I will stay on." Just months after the interview, he was diagnosed with cancer. Six weeks later, he died.

Upon Goizueta's death, former president Jimmy Carter observed, "Perhaps no other corporate leader in modern times has so beautifully exemplified the American dream. He believed that in America, all things are possible. He lived that dream. And because of his extraordinary leadership skills, he helped thousands of others realize their dreams as well."

Goizueta's Legacy

The legacy left to the company by Goizueta is incredible. When he took over Coca-Cola in 1981, the company's value was $4 billion. Under Goizueta's leadership, it rose to $150 billion. That's an increase in value of more than 3,500 percent! Coca-Cola became the second most valuable corporation in America, ahead of the car makers, the oil companies, Microsoft, Wal-Mart, and all the rest. The only company more valuable was General Electric. Many of Coke's stockholders became millionaires many times over. Emory University in Atlanta, whose portfolio contains a large block of Coca-Cola stock, now has an endowment comparable to that of Harvard.

But high stock value wasn't the most significant thing Goizueta gave to the Coca-Cola company. Instead it was the way he left a legacy. When the CEO's death was announced, there was no panic among Coca-Cola stockholders. Paine Webber analyst Emanuel Goldman said that Goizueta "prepared the company for his not being there as well as any executive I've ever seen."

How did he do it? First, by making the company as strong as he possibly could. Second, by preparing a successor for the top position named Douglas Ivester. Mickey H. Gramig, writer for the *Atlanta Constitution,* reported, "Unlike some companies, which face a crisis when the top executive leaves or dies, Coca-Cola is expected to retain its status as one of the world's most admired corporations. Goizueta had groomed Ivester to follow his footsteps since the Georgia native's 1994 appointment to the company's No. 2 post. And as an indication of how strongly Wall Street felt about Coca-Cola's footings, the company's stock barely rippled six weeks ago when Goizueta was diagnosed with lung cancer."[1]

Doug Ivester, an accountant by training, started his career with Coca-Cola in 1979 as the assistant controller. Four years later, he was named chief financial officer. He was known for his exceptional financial creativity, and he was a major force in Goizueta's ability to revolutionize the company's approach to investment and the handling of debt. By 1989, Goizueta must have decided that Ivester had untapped potential, because he moved him out of his strictly financial role and sent him to Europe to obtain operating and international experience. A year later, Goizueta brought him back and named him president of Coca-Cola USA, where he oversaw expenditures and marketing. From there he continued to groom Ivester, and in 1994, there could be no doubt that Ivester would follow Goizueta into the top position. Goizueta made him president and chief operating officer.

What Roberto Goizueta did was very unusual. Few chief executives of companies today develop strong leaders and groom them to take over the organization. John S. Wood, a consultant at Egon Zehnder International Inc., has noted that "companies have not in the recent past been investing as heavily in bringing people up. If they're not able to grow them, they have to go get them." So why was Roberto Goizueta different? He knew the positive effect of mentoring firsthand.

Roberto Goizueta was born in Cuba and educated at Yale, where he earned a degree in chemical engineering. When he returned to Havana in 1954, he answered a newspaper ad for a bilingual chemist. The company hiring turned out to be Coca-Cola. By 1966, he had become vice president of technical research and development at the company's headquarters in Atlanta. He was the youngest man ever to hold such a position in the company. But in the early 1970s, something even more important happened. Robert W. Woodruff, the patriarch of Coca-Cola, took Goizueta under his wing and began developing him. In 1975, Goizueta became the executive vice president of the company's technical division and took on other corporate responsibilities, such as overseeing legal affairs. And in 1980, with Woodruff's blessing, Goizueta became president and chief operating officer. One year later he was the chairman and chief executive. The reason Goizueta so confidently selected, developed, and groomed a successor in the 1990s is that he was building on the legacy that he had received in the 1970s.

LEADERS WHO LEAVE A LEGACY
OF SUCCESSION . . .

Leaders who leave a legacy of succession for their organization do the following:

Lead the Organization with a "Long View"

Just about anybody can make an organization look good for a moment—by launching a flashy new program or product, drawing crowds to a big event, or slashing the budget to boost the bottom line. But leaders who leave a legacy take a different approach. They lead with tomorrow as well as today in mind. That's what Goizueta did. He planned to keep leading as long as he was effective, yet he prepared his successor anyway. He always looked out for the best interests of the organization and its stockholders.

Create a Leadership Culture

The most stable companies have strong leaders at every level of the organization. The only way to develop such widespread leadership is to make developing leaders a part of your culture. That is a strong part of Coca-Cola's legacy. How many other successful companies do you know about that have had a succession of leaders come up within the ranks of their own organization?

Pay the Price Today to Assure Success Tomorrow

There is no success without sacrifice. Each organization is unique, and that dictates what the price will be. But any leader who wants to help his organization must be willing to pay that price to ensure lasting success.

VALUE TEAM LEADERSHIP ABOVE
INDIVIDUAL LEADERSHIP

No matter how good he is, no leader can do it all alone. Just as in sports a coach needs a team of good players to win, an organization needs a team of good *leaders* to succeed. The larger the organization, the stronger, larger, and deeper the team of leaders needs to be.

WALK AWAY FROM THE ORGANIZATION
WITH INTEGRITY

In the case of Coca-Cola, the leader didn't get the opportunity to walk away because he died an untimely death. But if he had lived, I believe Goizueta would have done just that. When it's a leader's time to leave the organization, he has got to be willing to walk away and let his successor do his own thing. Meddling only hurts him and the organization.

FEW LEADERS PASS IT ON

Max Dupree, author of *Leadership Is an Art,* declared, "Succession is one of the key responsibilities of leadership." Yet of all the characteristics of leadership, legacy is the one that the fewest leaders seem to learn. Achievement comes to someone when he is able to do great things for himself. Success comes when he empowers followers to do great things *with* him. Significance comes when he develops leaders to do great things *for* him. But a legacy is created only when a person puts his organization into the position to do great things *without* him.

I learned the importance of legacy the hard way. Because the church grew so much while I was in my first leadership position in Hillham, Indiana, I thought I was a success. When I began there, we had only three people in attendance. For three years, I built up that church, reached out to the community, and influenced many people's lives. When I left, our average attendance was in the high two hundreds, and our record was more than three hundred people. I had programs in place, and everything looked rosy to me. I thought I had really done something significant.

Eighteen months after I had moved to my second church, I had lunch with a friend I hadn't seen in a while, and he had just spent some time in Hillham. I asked him about how things were going back there, and I was surprised to hear his answer.

"Not too good," he answered.

"Really?" I said. "Why? Things were going great when I left. What's wrong?"

"Well," he said, "it's kind of fallen off. Some of the programs you got started kind of petered out. The church is running only about a hundred people. It might get even smaller before it's all over."

That really bothered me. A leader hates to see something that he put his sweat, blood, and tears into starting to fail. At first, I got ticked off at the leader who followed me. But then it hit me. If I had done a really good job there, it wouldn't matter what kind of leader followed me, good or bad. The fault was really mine. I hadn't set up the organization to succeed after I left. It was the first time I realized the significance of legacy.

PARADIGM SHIFT

After that, I started to look at leadership in a whole new way. Every leader eventually leaves his organization—one way or another. He may change jobs, get promoted, or retire. And even if a person refuses to retire, he is going to die. That made me realize that part of my job as a leader was to start preparing my people and organization for what inevitably lies ahead. That prompted me to change my focus from leading followers to developing leaders. My lasting value, like that of any leader, would be measured by my ability to give the organization a smooth succession.

My best personal succession story concerns my departure from Skyline Church. When I first arrived there in 1981, I made one of my primary goals the identification and development of leaders because I knew that our success depended on it. Over the fourteen years I was there, my staff and I developed literally hundreds of outstanding leaders, both volunteers and staff.

One of my greatest joys in life is knowing that Skyline is stronger now than when I left in 1995. Jim Garlow, who succeeded me as the senior pastor, is doing a wonderful job there. In the fall of 1997, Jim asked me to come back to Skyline and speak at a fund-raising banquet for the next phase of the building project, and I was delighted to honor his request.

About 4,100 people attended the event at the San Diego Convention Center, located on the city's beautiful bay. My wife, Margaret, and I really enjoyed the chance to see and talk with so many of our old friends. And of course, I felt privileged to be the evening's keynote speaker. It was quite a celebration—and quite a success. People pledged more than $7.8 million toward the building of the church's new facility.

As soon as I finished speaking, Margaret and I slipped out of the ballroom. We wanted the night to belong to Jim, since he was now the leader of Skyline. Because of that, we knew it would be best if we made a quick exit before the program was over. Descending the stairs, I grabbed her hand and gave it a squeeze. It was wonderful to know that what we started all those years ago was still going on. It's like my friend Chris Musgrove says, "Success is not measured by what you're leaving to, but by what you are leaving behind."

When all is said and done, your ability as a leader will not be judged by what you achieved personally or even by what your team accomplished during your tenure. You will be judged by how well your people and your organization did after you were gone. Your lasting value will be measured by succession.

Notes

Chapter 1
1. John F. Love, *McDonald's: Behind the Arches* (New York: Bantam Books, 1986).

Chapter 2
1. "The Champ," *Reader's Digest*, January 1972, 109.

Chapter 3
1. Quoted at www.abcnews.com on 4 February 1998.
2. Thomas A. Stewart, "Brain Power: Who Owns It . . . How They Profit from It," *Fortune*, 17 March 1997, 105–6.

Chapter 4
1. Robert Dilenschneider, *Power and Influence: Mastering the Art of Persuasion* (New York: Prentice Hall, 1990).
2. E. C. McKenzie, *Quips and Quotes* (Grand Rapids: Baker, 1980).
3. Fred Smith, *Learning to Lead* (Waco: Word, 1986), 117.
4. John C. Maxwell, *Be a People Person* (Wheaton: Victor, 1989).

Chapter 6
1. R. Earl Allen, *Let It Begin in Me* (Nashville: Broadman Press, 1985).

Chapter 7
1. E. M. Swift, "Odd Man Out," *Sports Illustrated*, 92–96.
2. Robert Shaw, "Tough Trust," *Leader to Leader* (Winter 1997), 46–54.

Chapter 10
1. Mickey H. Gramig, *Atlanta Constitution*, 10 November 1997.

Books by Dr. John C. Maxwell
Can Teach You How to Be a REAL Success

RELATIONSHIPS

Be a People Person (Victor Books)
Becoming a Person of Influence (Thomas Nelson)
The Power of Influence (Honor Books)
The Power of Partnership in the Church (J. Countryman)
The Treasure of a Friend (J. Countryman)

EQUIPPING

The 17 Indisputable Laws of Teamwork (Thomas Nelson)
The 17 Essential Qualities of a Team Player (Thomas Nelson)
Developing the Leaders Around You (Thomas Nelson)
Partners in Prayer (Thomas Nelson)
Success One Day at a Time (J. Countryman)

ATTITUDE

Be All You Can Be (Victor Books)
Failing Forward (Thomas Nelson)
The Power of Thinking (Honor Books)
Living at the Next Level (Thomas Nelson)
Think on These Things (Beacon Hill)]
The Winning Attitude (Thomas Nelson)
Your Bridge to a Better Future (Thomas Nelson)
The Power of Attitude (Honor Books)

LEADERSHIP

The 21 Indispensable Qualities of a Leader (Thomas Nelson)
The 21 Irrefutable Laws of Leadership (Thomas Nelson)
The 21 Most Powerful Minutes in a Leader's Day (Thomas Nelson)
Developing the Leader Within You (Thomas Nelson)
The Power of Leadership (Honor Books)
The Right to Lead (J. Countryman)
Your Road Map for Success (Thomas Nelson)

John Maxwell's REAL Leadership Series

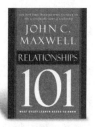

Relationships 101
ISBN 0-7852-6351-9

Available Fall 2003

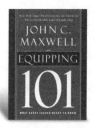

Equipping 101
ISBN 0-7852-6352-7

Available Winter 2004

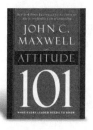

Attitude 101
ISBN 0-7852-6350-0

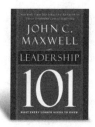

Leadership 101
ISBN 0-7852-6419-1

THOMAS NELSON
PUBLISHERS
Since 1798

CONTINUE

We hope you've enjoyed *Leadership 101* and we want you to know that at INJOY® leadership is what we're all about. We are dedicated to developing you as a leader of excellence and integrity by providing the finest resources and training for your personal and professional growth.

YOUR  **Leadership** Wired

Take the next step in developing the leadership potential in yourself and in those around you. We've made the first step as simple and as inexpensive as possible — it's FREE and it's delivered to your email box twice a month! Visit www.Leadership101book.com and sign up for *Leadership Wired* today!

LEADERSHIP

Ready for a challenge that's a little meatier? We recommend *The 21 Irrefutable Laws of Leadership*. Read this *New York Times'* best-seller and you'll take that next giant step toward becoming the leader you've always wanted to be. Order online today at www.Leadership101book.com.

EDUCATION!

 Visit **www.Leadership101book.com** and sign up for your FREE subscription to *Leadership Wired* today!

SHARE THESE

If you've found valuable leadership insights within the pages of *Leadership 101,* why not share this treasure with friends, family, and business associates? Visit us at www.Leadership101book.com and order a copy for those you value!

LEADERSHIP

Great for holidays, anniversaries, and birthdays, let *Leadership 101* show those closest to you that you care about their personal and professional growth. Also, for you sales leaders, remember that *Leadership 101* makes for a great sales leave behind! Order today at www.Leadership101book.com.

LESSONS

Do you have children preparing to leave home for college, the military, or the business world? Give them a headstart on an incredible competitive advantage — leadership! Visit us at www.Leadership101book.com and order them a copy of *Leadership 101* today.

WITH FRIENDS!

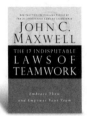

THE 17 INDISPUTABLE LAWS OF TEAMWORK

Everyone who works with people is realizing that the old autocratic method of leadership simply doesn't work. The way to win is to build a great team.

John C. Maxwell has been teaching the benefits of leadership and team building for years. Now he tackles the importance of teamwork head on, writing about teamwork being necessary for every kind of leader, and showing how team building can improve every area of your life.

ISBN 0-7852-7434-0

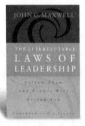

THE 21 IRREFUTABLE LAWS OF LEADERSHIP

What would happen if a top expert with more than thirty years of leadership experience were willing to distill everything he had learned about leadership into a handful of life-changing principles for you? It would change your life.

John C. Maxwell has done exactly that in *The 21 Irrefutable Laws of Leadership*. He has combined insights learned from his thirty-plus years of leadership successes and mistakes with observations from the worlds of business, politics, sports, religion, and military conflict. The result is a revealing study of leadership delivered as only a communicator like Maxwell can.

ISBN 0-7852-7431-6

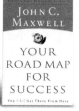

YOUR ROAD MAP FOR SUCCESS

Defining success is a difficult task. Most people equate it with wealth, power, and happiness. However, true success is not a thing you acquire or achieve. Rather, it is a journey you take your whole life long. In a refreshingly straightforward style, John Maxwell shares unique insights into what it means to be successful. And he reveals a definition that puts genuine success within your reach yet motivates you to keep striving for your dreams.

ISBN 0-7852-6596-1

THOMAS NELSON
PUBLISHERS
Since 1798

About the Author

Known as America's expert on leadership, JOHN C. MAXWELL is founder of the INJOY Group™, an organization dedicated to helping people maximize their personal and leadership potential. Through his seminars, books, and tapes, Dr. Maxwell encourages, teaches, and motivates more than one million people each year. He has authored more than twenty-five books, including bestsellers *The 21 Irrefutable Laws of Leadership, The 21 Indispensable Qualities of a Leader, Developing the Leader Within You, The 17 Indisputable Laws of Teamwork, Your Road Map for Success* and *Failing Forward.*